VISION BOARD
FOR BLACK WOMEN

A COMPREHENSIVE DREAM COLLAGE MAGAZINE &
VISION BOARD CLIP ART BOOK WITH 600+ MOTIVATIONAL
IMAGES, AFFIRMATIONS & CREATIVE ART SUPPLIES
FOR MANIFESTING SUCCESS

Copyright © 2024 by K & A Publishing. All rights reserved. No portion of this book may be reproduced in any form without written permission from the publisher or author, except as permitted by U.S. copyright law.

Some images courtesy of: vecteezy.com, freepik.com, pixabay.com, pexels.com

Visualize Your Ideal Future: A Comprehensive Vision Board Guide for Black Women

Welcome to your transformative journey of self-discovery and goal achievement. This guide is designed to help you harness the power of visualization and turn your aspirations into reality.

Within these pages, you'll find a wealth of resources to guide you through creating a vision board that reflects your deepest ambitions and desires. This isn't just about arranging images on a board; it's about crafting a visual representation of the life you aspire to lead.

Our comprehensive guide includes over 100 pages of inspiring imagery, thought-provoking quotes, and practical exercises. Each section is tailored to address key areas of adult life:

1. Personal Growth: Enhance your confidence, overcome obstacles, and cultivate a growth mindset.

2. Body Positivity & Self-Love: Develop a deep sense of self-worth and love for which you truly are and enhance your unique qualities.

3. Health & Fitness: Set wellness goals, find workout motivation, and embrace holistic health practices.

4. Career & Professional Development: Map out your career trajectory, set ambitious professional goals, and plan for success.

5. Financial Goals: Visualize financial freedom, set savings targets, and plan for long-term wealth.

6. Mental Wellness & Emotional Balance: Learn to manage stress, navigate your emotions with mindfulness, and develop healthy coping strategies.

7. Spirituality & Mindfulness: Explore practices for inner peace, self-awareness, and spiritual growth.

8. Style & Fashion: Discover your personal style, experiment with bold choices, and use fashion as a powerful tool to express your unique personality and boost your self-confidence.

9. Travel & Adventure: Plan dream vacations, set adventure goals, and expand your cultural horizons.

10. Education & Learning: Set lifelong learning objectives and plan for personal and professional growth.

11. Creative Expression: Tap into your artistic side and set goals for creative projects.

12. Artistic & Creative Pursuits: Explore your imagination, dive into new artistic endeavors to fuel your passion, relieve stress, and bring your visions to life.

13. Home & Family: Envision your ideal living space and the lifestyle you desire.

14. Parenting & Family Planning: Build meaningful connections, and create a supportive. An environment that encourages growth, love, and understanding within your family.

15. Relationships & Love: Strengthen bonds, improve communication, and envision harmonious relationships.

16. Friendships & Social Life: Build lasting friendships, and create a vibrant social circle that brings joy, trust, and a sense of belonging into your life.

17. Home Décor & Living Spaces: Design a living space that reflects your personality, and enhances your well-being by transforming your home into a haven of style and serenity.

18. Community & Social Impact: Visualize ways to contribute to your community and make a positive impact.

19. Leadership & Influence: Develop strong leadership skills, lead by example, and cultivate the ability to motivate and influence those around you to achieve shared goals and personal growth.

20. Work-Life & Balance: Strive to maintain a healthy equilibrium between professional responsibilities and personal life. Set clear boundaries, and practice self-care to ensure productivity and well-being.

21. Hobbies & Interests: Rediscover passions or explore new interests that bring joy and fulfillment.

22. Environmental Consciousness: Set eco-friendly goals and visualize a sustainable lifestyle.

PREPARING YOUR MINDSET

Before diving into the creative process, take a moment to align your mindset:

1. Embrace Openness:
Approach this process with an open mind, believing in your power to shape your future.

2. Commit to Growth:
Be willing to challenge self-imposed limitations and see your true potential.

3. Engage Your Imagination:
Recognize the power of visualization in manifesting your desires.

4. Cultivate Curiosity:
Approach each activity with eagerness to learn more about yourself.

5. Connect with Your Aspirations:
Use this guide to uncover your deepest passions and most ambitious dreams.

With your mind open and ready, let's dive in and start creating the life you really want to live!

CREATING YOUR VISION BOARD: A STEP-BY-STEP APPROACH

To get the most out of this book, follow these steps:

1. Define Your Objectives: Clarify your goals and let them guide your process.

2. Explore the Contents: Familiarize yourself with the various sections and themes.

3. Select Your Focus: Choose areas that resonate most with your current life stage and aspirations.

4. Engage Deeply: Reflect on the quotes, prompts, and wisdom provided.

5. Visualize: Use the provided imagery and affirmations to bring your goals to life visually.

6. Reflect & Document: Take time to journal about your insights and realizations.

7. Take Action: Develop concrete steps to move towards your visualized goals.

8. Revisit and Revise: Return to your vision board regularly for inspiration and updates.

9. Share Your Journey: Inspire others by sharing your experiences and creations.

10. Celebrate Progress: Acknowledge your achievements and growth along the way.

By embracing this journey, you're taking a powerful step towards manifesting the life you desire. Let this guide be your compass as you navigate the path to personal fulfillment and success.

Your aspirations deserve to be visualized – let this vision board guide be your catalyst for transformation.

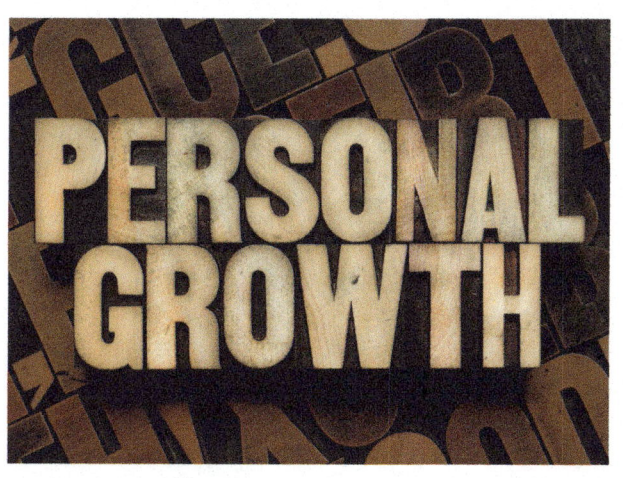

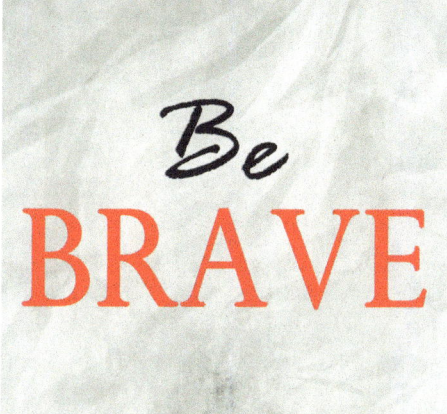

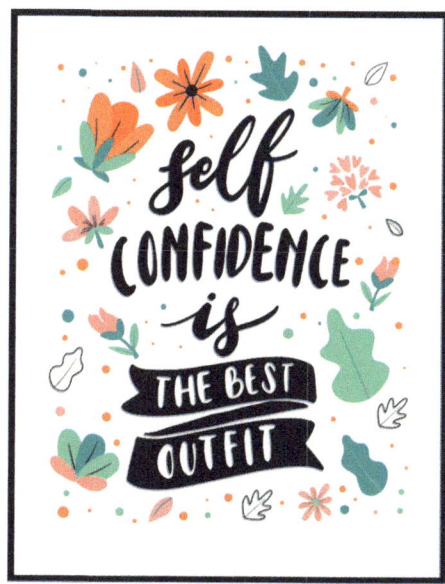

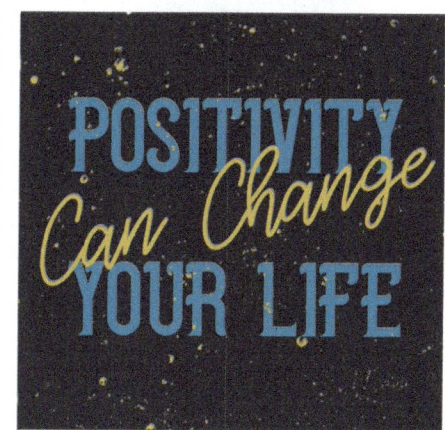

I am Resilient BECAUSE I RISE ABOVE EVERY CHALLENGE	**I am Empowered** BECAUSE I TRUST MY INNER STRENGTH
I am Successful BECAUSE I WORK HARD & STAY FOCUSED	**I am Joyful** BECAUSE I CHOOSE GRATITUDE EVERY DAY
I am Courageous BECAUSE I FACE MY FEARS WITH DETERMINATION	**I am Radiant** BECAUSE I EMBRACE MY UNIQUE BEAUTY
I am Peaceful BECAUSE I NURTURE MY MENTAL WELL-BEING	**I am Creative** BECAUSE I ALLOW MY IMAGINATION TO FLOW FREELY
I am Inspired BECAUSE I FOLLOW MY PASSIONS WHOLEHEARTEDLY	**I am Adventurous** BECAUSE I WELCOME NEW EXPERIENCES WITH AN OPEN HEART
I am Fearless BECAUSE I STEP BOLDLY INTO THE UNKNOWN	**I am Balanced** BECAUSE I CREATE HARMONY IN MY WORK & PERSONAL LIFE

UNIQUE GLOW

SELF ACCEPTANCE

SELF-CARE is not a luxury, it is a necessity.

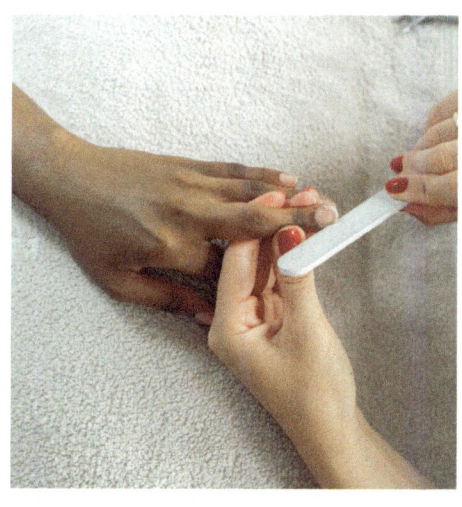

> **Beauty** begins the moment you decide to be yourself.
> *Coco Chanel*

TRANSFORMATION

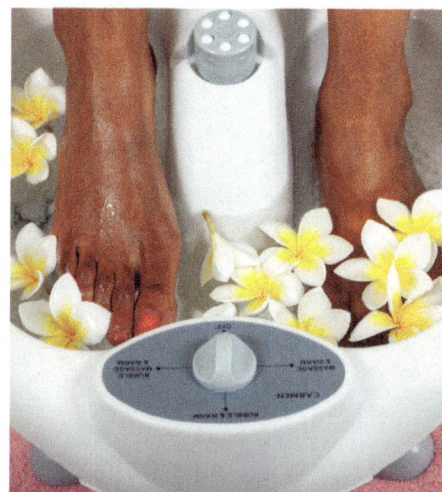

- ROYAL ESSENCE
- MELANIN MAGIC
- ANCESTRAL WISDOM
- UNAPOLOGETIC
- LEGACY BUILDER
- QUEENDOM
- ALIGNED
- ABUNDANT JOY
- RADIANT POWER
- PURPOSEFUL
- LIMITLESS HORIZONS
- DIVINE FEMININE
- ROOTED POWER
- PROTECTED PEACE
- BOSS MOVES
- BLACK EXCELLENCE
- UNSTOPPABLE FORCE
- CULTURAL IMPACT
- ETERNAL LIGHT

ENERGY STRENGTH

BALANCE

VITALITY

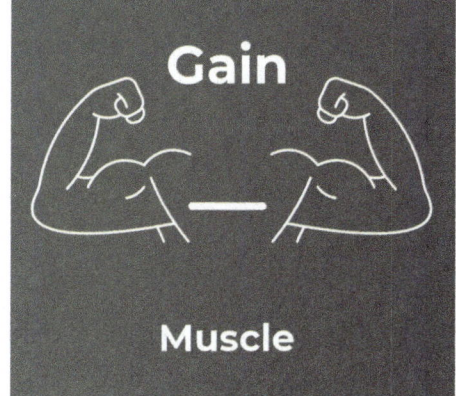

VIBRANT WELLNESS

OPTIMIAL LIVING

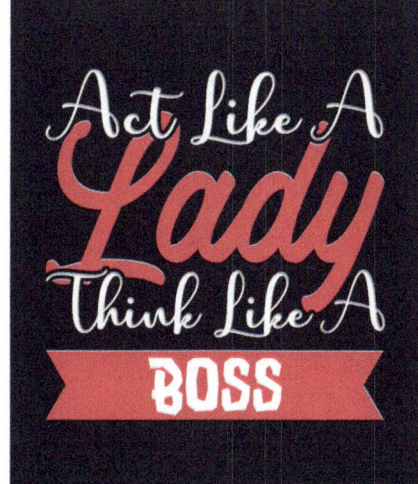

Passion is the difference between having a job and having a *Career*

LIFE SKILLS

Good Presenters Are Storytellers

Money is the sixth sense that makes it possible to enjoy the other five.

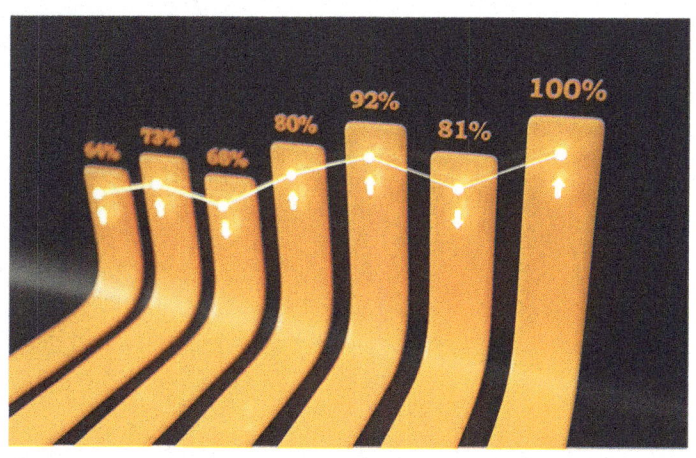

FINANCIAL FREEDOM

CREATE MULTIPLE STREAMS OF INCOME

PROSPERITY

ABUNDANCE

Bank of Abundance & Wealth

Date: _____

PAY TO THE ORDER OF: _____

$ [   ]

_____ Dollars

Memo: _____

_____
Authorized Signature

0123456 789 345678901

Bank of Abundance & Wealth

Date: _____

PAY TO THE ORDER OF: _____

£ [   ]

_____ Pounds

Memo: _____

_____
Authorised Signature

0123456 789 345678901

Bank of Abundance & Wealth

Date: _____

PAY TO THE ORDER OF: _____

$ [   ]

_____ Dollars

Memo: _____

_____
Authorized Signature

0123456 789 345678901

MENTAL HEALTH MATTERS

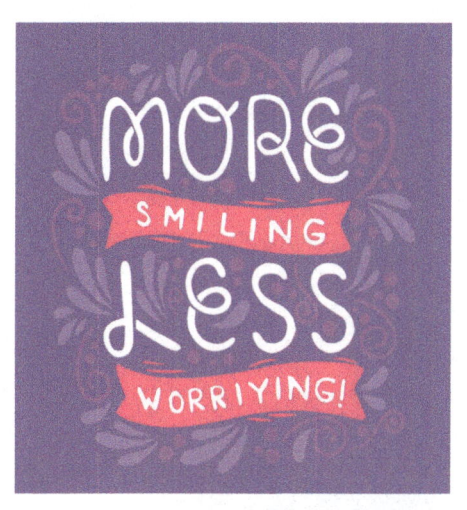

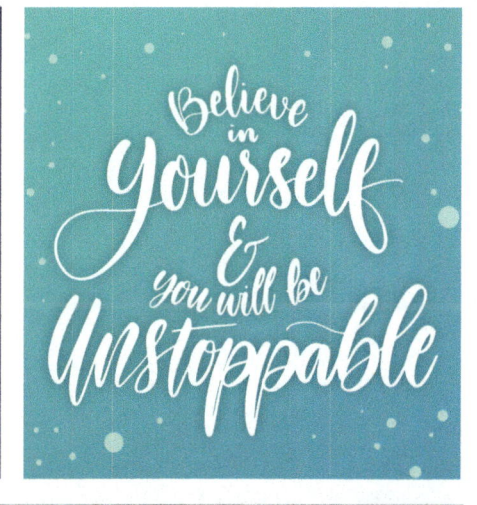

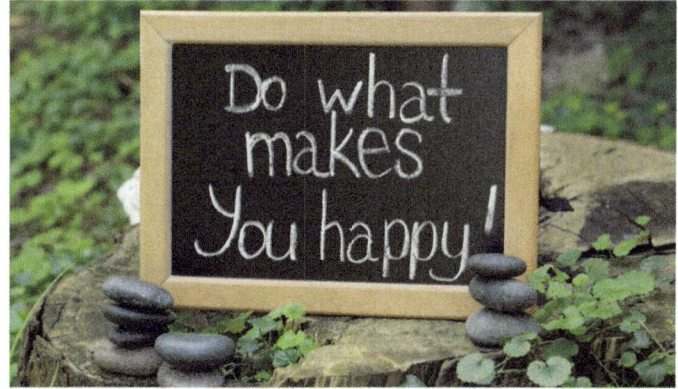

Every new day is another chance to change your life

MORE SMILING LESS WORRIYING!

HAPPY MIND HAPPY LIFE

I can and I will.

Believe in Yourself & you will be Unstoppable

YOU ARE BEAUTIFUL

Do what makes you happy!

MINDFULNESS **GRATITUDE**

trust

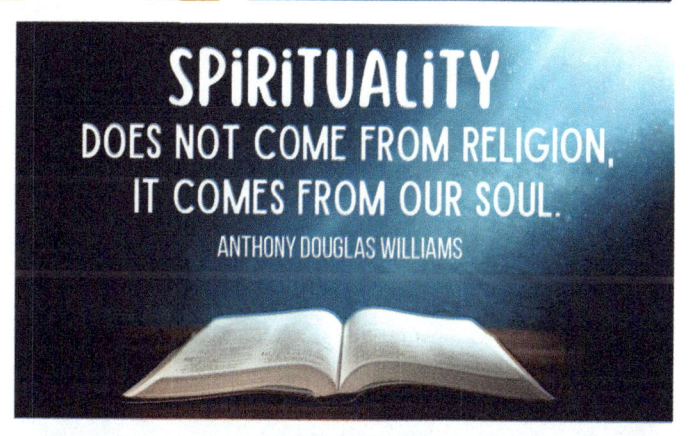

MEDITATION HELPS YOUR Mind

SPIRITUALITY DOES NOT COME FROM RELIGION, IT COMES FROM OUR SOUL.
ANTHONY DOUGLAS WILLIAMS

KEEP CALM

PATIENCE

Faith

EVERYTHING IS POSSIBLE WITH GOD.
MARK 10:27

Hope

BELIEVE

LIFTING OTHERS LIFTS YOU

PRAISE

HARMONY

GOD LOVES YOU

- EVERY STEP I TAKE IS A STEP TOWARD MY HIGHEST POTENTIAL.
- I AM WORTHY OF LOVE & ACCEPTANCE, JUST AS I AM.
- MY BODY IS STRONG, HEALTHY, & FULL OF ENERGY.
- I ATTRACT ABUNDANCE & MAKE WISE FINANCIAL CHOICES.
- MY PERSONAL STYLE REFLECTS MY CONFIDENCE & INDIVIDUALITY.
- ADVENTURE FILLS MY LIFE WITH EXCITEMENT & GROWTH.
- I AM EAGER TO LEARN & EXPAND MY KNOWLEDGE.
- I EXPRESS MY IDEAS BOLDLY & FEARLESSLY.
- MY HOME IS A SANCTUARY OF LOVE, JOY, & PEACE.
- I CHOOSE HABITS THAT NOURISH & SUPPORT MY WELL-BEING.
- I AM BUILDING A SUCCESSFUL & FULFILLING CAREER.
- I RELEASE NEGATIVITY & WELCOME BALANCE & JOY.

BOLDNESS

ELEGANCE

Style is a simple way of saying complicated things.

STUNNING

EXQUISITE

Travel

LET'S GO TRAVEL

to travel is to live

I **TRAVEL**
BECAUSE DISTANCE & DIFFERENCE ARE THE
SECRET TONIC TO CREATIVITY.

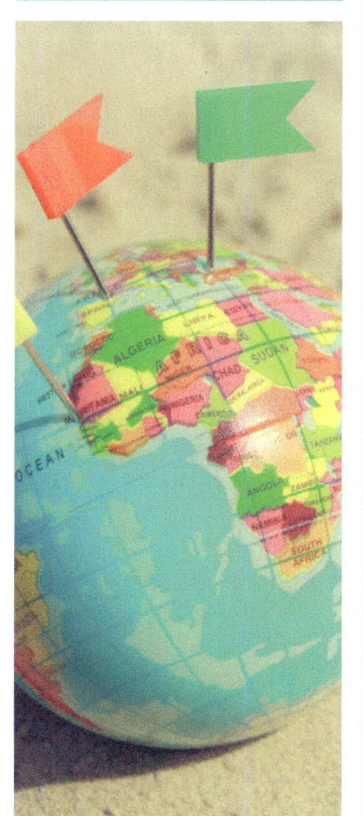

Adventure Awaits,

Go, find it.

EIFFEL TOWER (FRANCE)	STONEHENGE (ENGLAND)	GREAT WALL OF CHINA
CHICHEN ITZA (MEXICO)	BOARDWALK ISLAND RESORT (MALDIVES)	OYA SANTORINI (GREECE)
PYRAMIDS OF GIZA (EGYPT)	SAGRADA PALACE BARCELONA (SPAIN)	VENICE (ITALY)
SYDNEY OPERA HOUSE (AUSTRALIA)	NIAGARA FALLS (CANADA)	TAJ MAHAL (INDIA)
CHOBH NATIONAL PARK (BOTSWANA)	PETRA THE TREASURY (JORDAN)	HISTORY MUSEUM VIENNA (AUSTRIA)

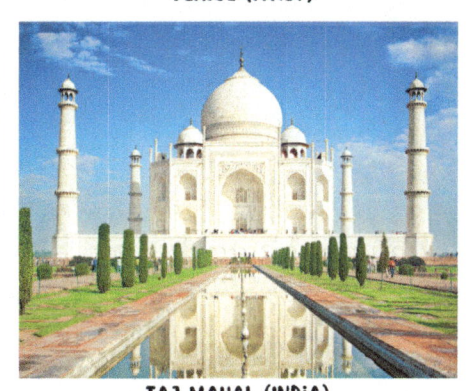

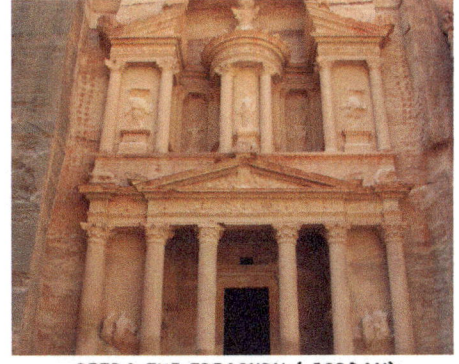

WATER PARK PATTAYA (THAILAND)	 OKINAWA CHURAUMI AQUARIUM (JAPAN)	 BLUE MOSQUE ISTANBUL (TURKEY)
 TAMAN AYUN TEMPLE BALI (INDONESIA)	 CHAPEL BRIDGE LUCERNE (SWITZERLAND)	 MURILLO SQUARE LA PAZ (BOLIVIA)
 CABLE STAYED BRIDGE SÃO PAULO (BRAZIL)	 CINQUANTENAIRE, BRUSSELS (BELGIUM)	 BERLINER DOM, BERLIN (GERMANY)
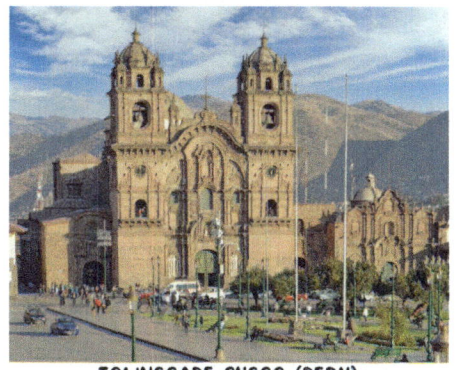 TOWNSCAPE CUSCO (PERU)	 BURJ AL ARAB DUBAI (UAE)	 PUBLIC SQUARE LISBON (PORTUGAL)
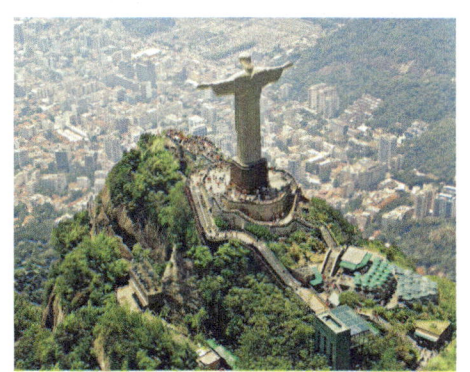 CHRIST THE REDEEMER (BRAZIL)	 SANTA CLAUS VILLAGE ROVANIEMI (FINLAND)	 WALLED CITY DUBROVNIK, (CROATIA)

BOARDING PASS

COMPANYNAME   COMPANYNAME

Name of passenger   Date   Time

Class   Gate   Seat

From   Destination

Flight

WWW.COMPANYNAME.COM

NAME
LASTNAME
FROM
TO
FLIGHT
SEAT

FOR CANCELATE OR CHANGE
WWW.COMPANYNAME.COM

BOARDING PASS

FIRST CLASS

NAME:
FLIGHT:
DATE:
TIME:
GATE:
SEAT:

NAME:
FROM:
TO:

FLIGHT:
GATE:
NAME:
FROM:
TO:

Boarding Pass
First Class

First Class

NAME OF PASSANGER: FLIGHT: NAME OF PASSANGER:

FROM: GATE: SEAT: FLIGHT: GATE:

TO: DATE:

BOARDING: BOARDING:

DATE: N°. 44586-65455321BDA

GATE CLOSES 30 MINUTES BEFORE DEPARTURE

BCRN-8456.2235

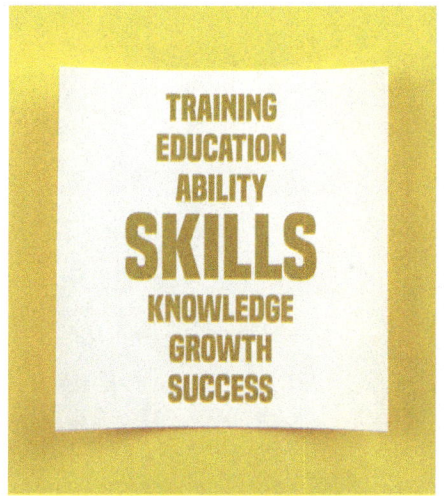

TRAINING
EDUCATION
ABILITY
SKILLS
KNOWLEDGE
GROWTH
SUCCESS

E-LEARNING
online education

LEARN NEW SKILLS

NEVER STOP LEARNING

LEARN A NEW LANGUAGE
1.
2.
3.

IF YOU ARE NOT WILLING TO LEARN, **LEARN,** NO ONE CAN HELP YOU. IF YOU ARE DETERMINED TO LEARN NO ONE CAN **STOP** YOU.

Each day I learn something new.

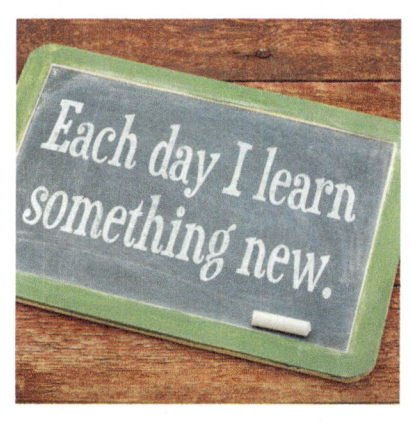

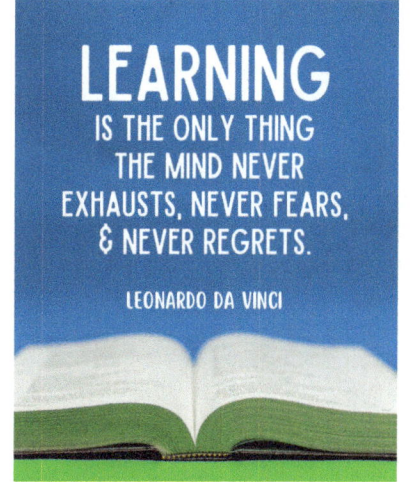

READ MORE

LEARNING IS THE ONLY THING THE MIND NEVER EXHAUSTS, NEVER FEARS, & NEVER REGRETS.

LEONARDO DA VINCI

CURIOSITY

WISDOM

Knowledge is power.

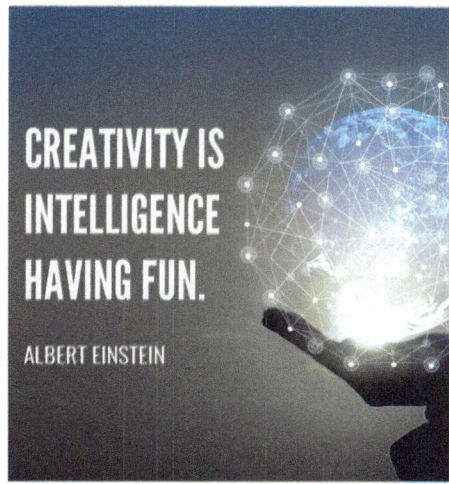

CREATIVITY IS INTELLIGENCE HAVING FUN.
ALBERT EINSTEIN

INSPIRATION

IMAGINATION

Sweet Home

HOME IS WHERE YOUR SOUL RESTS.

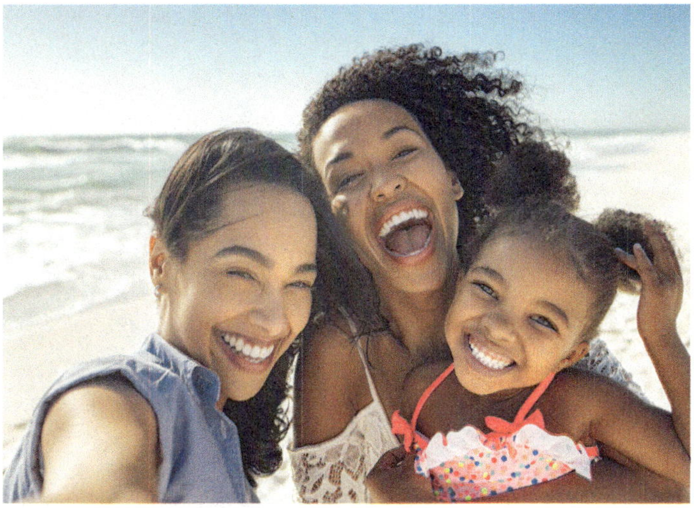
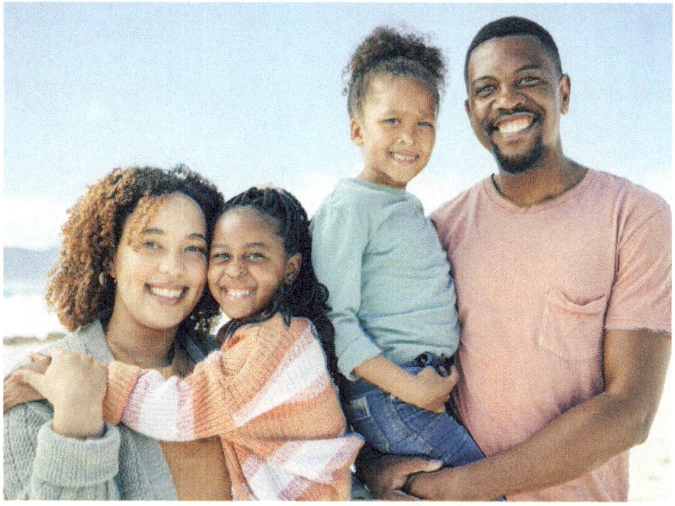
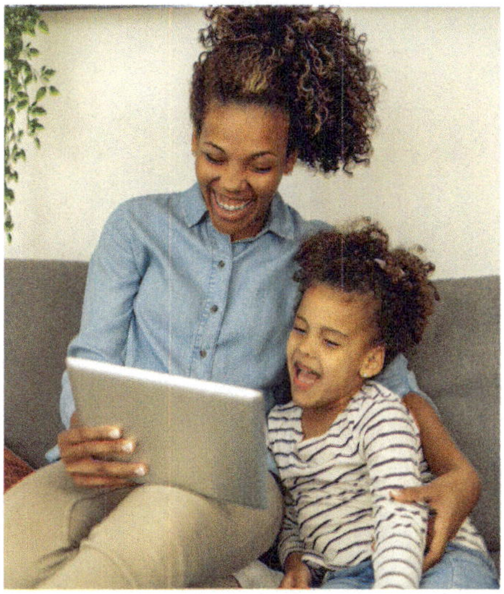
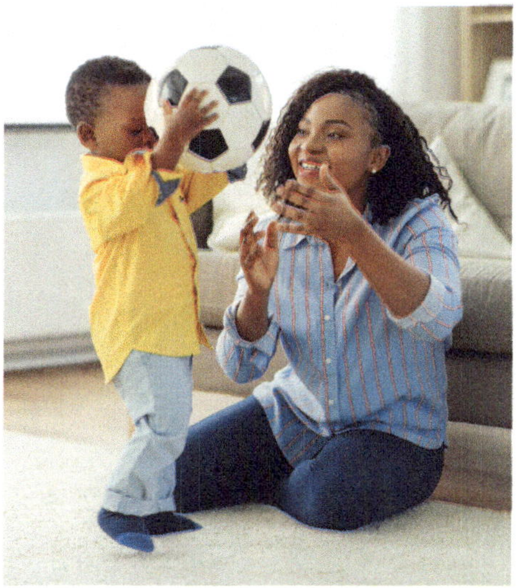
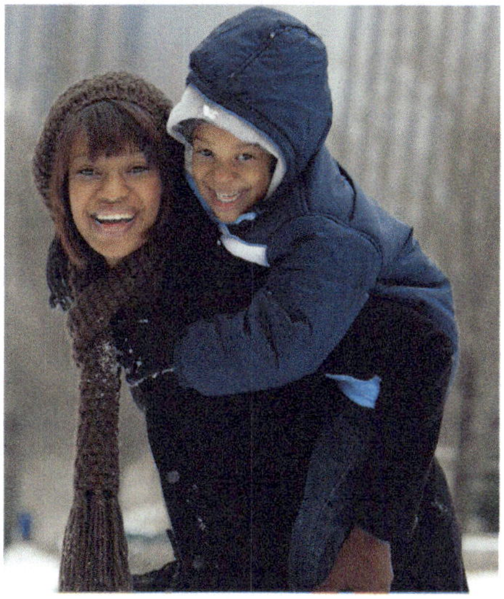
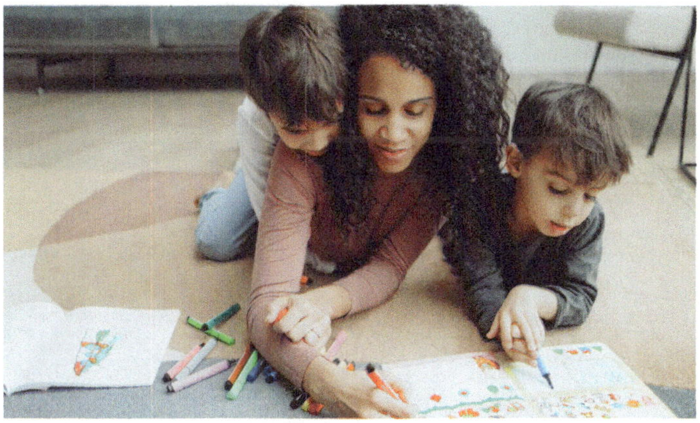
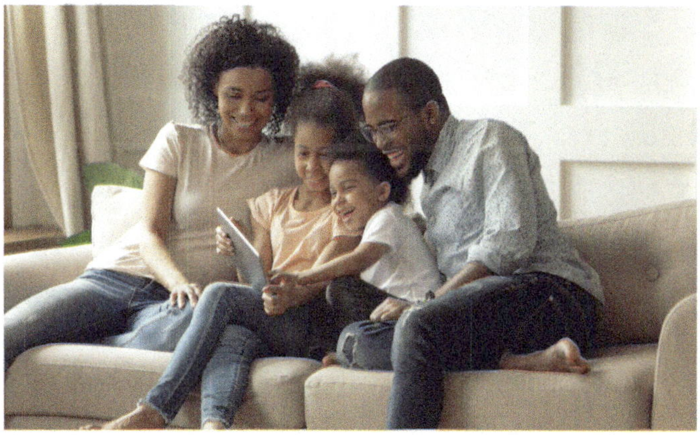
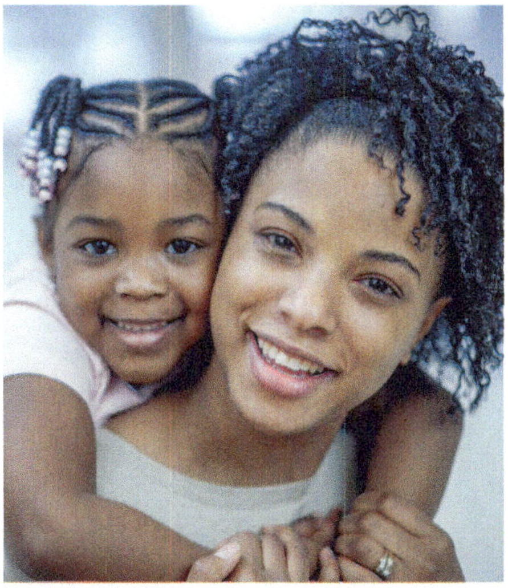
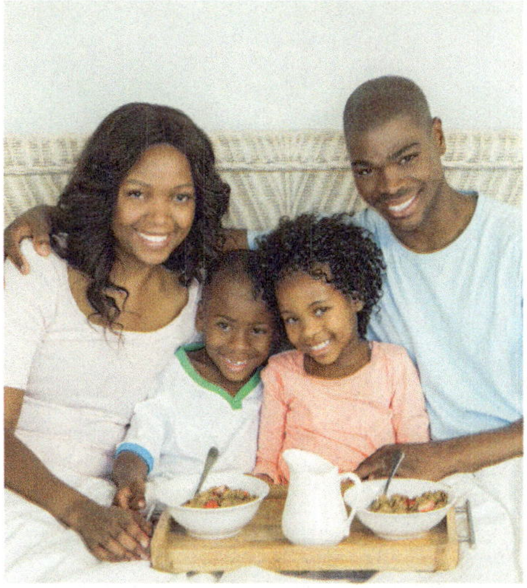
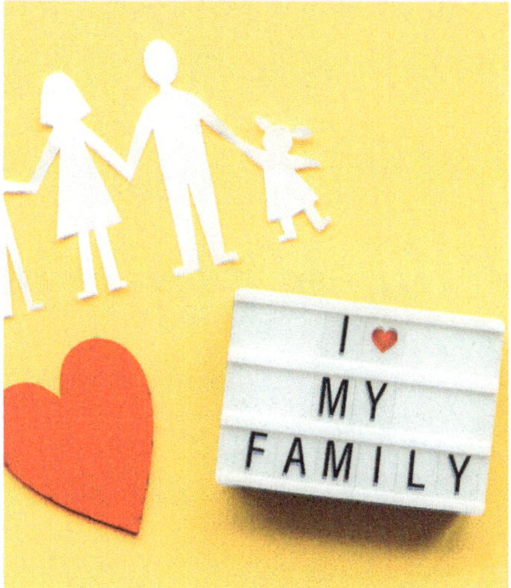
I ♥
MY
FAMILY

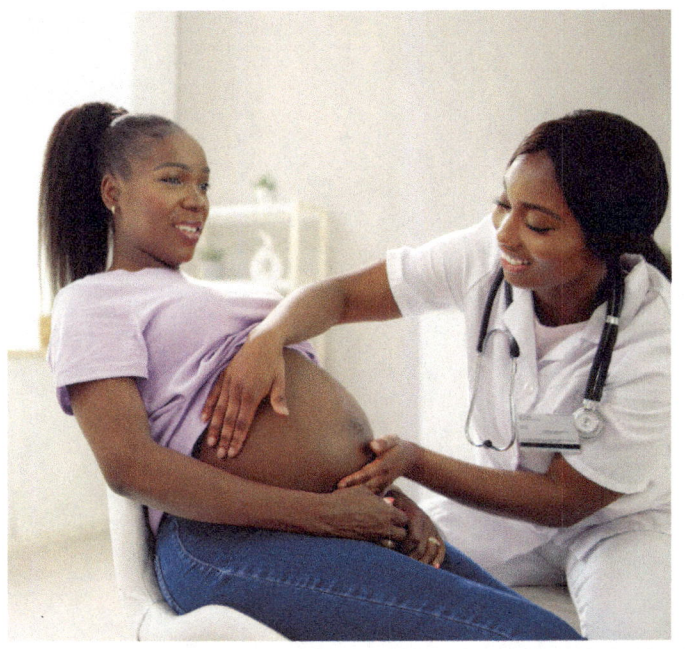

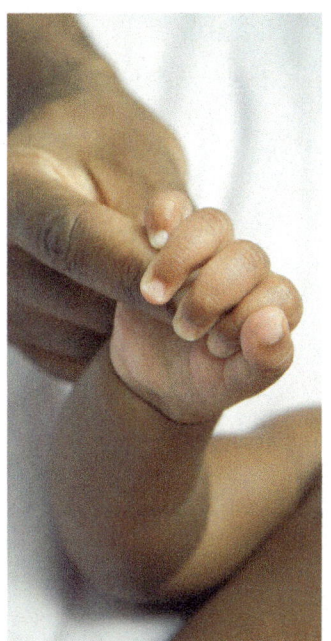

BEST MOM EVER

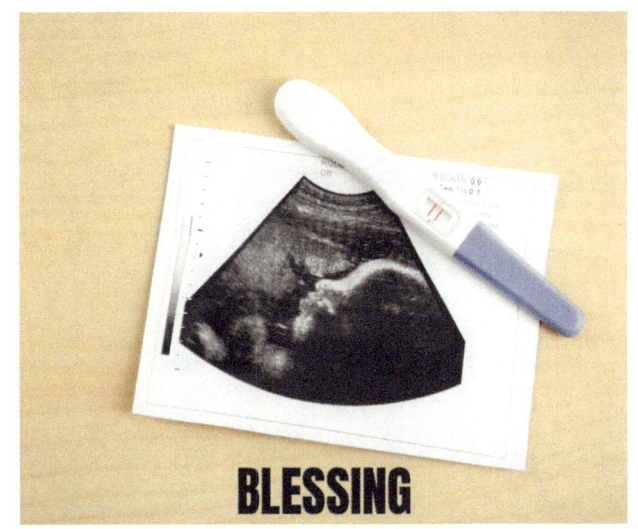

THE MOST MAGICAL DAY OF MY LIFE WAS THE DAY I BECAME A *mother*

BLESSING

MY L♥VE JUST FOR Y♥U

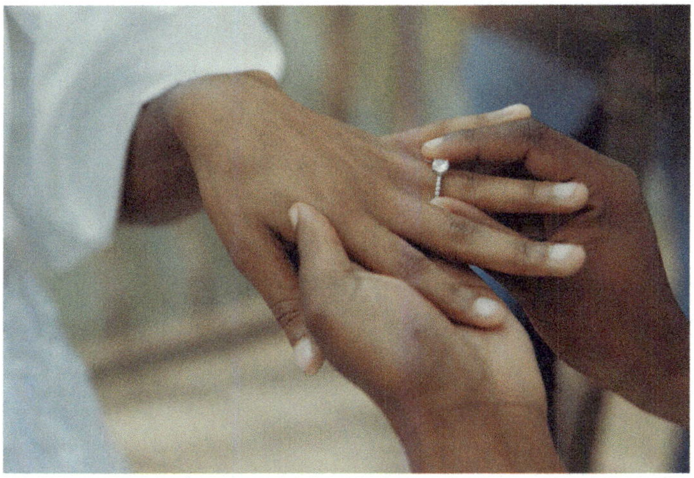

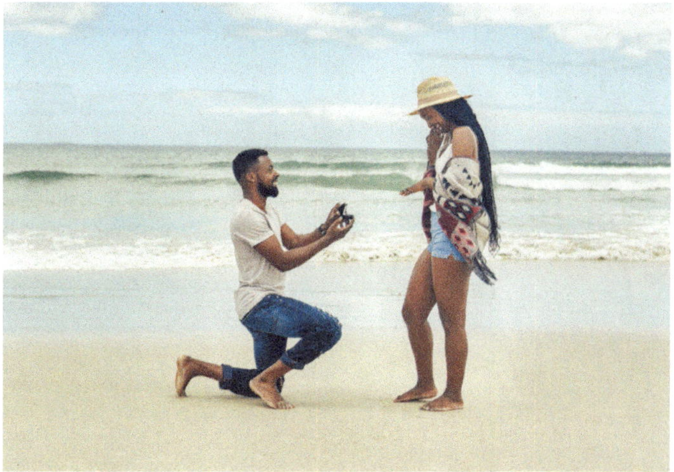

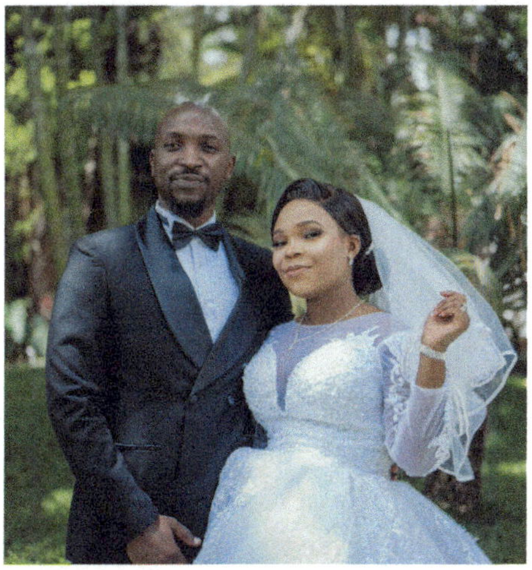

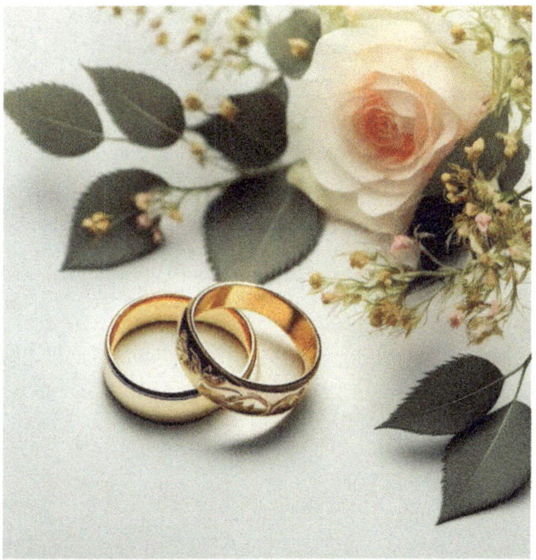

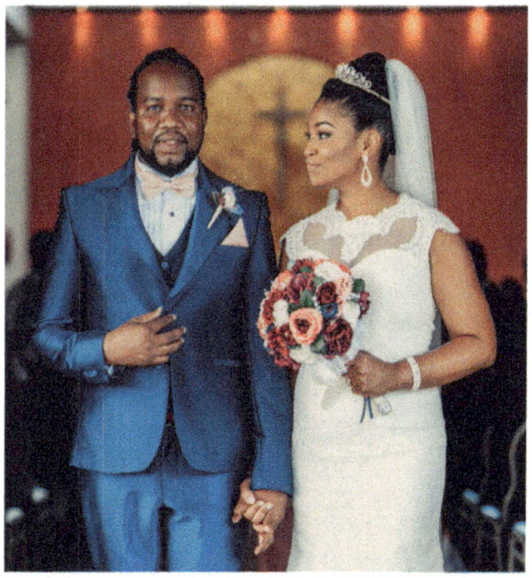

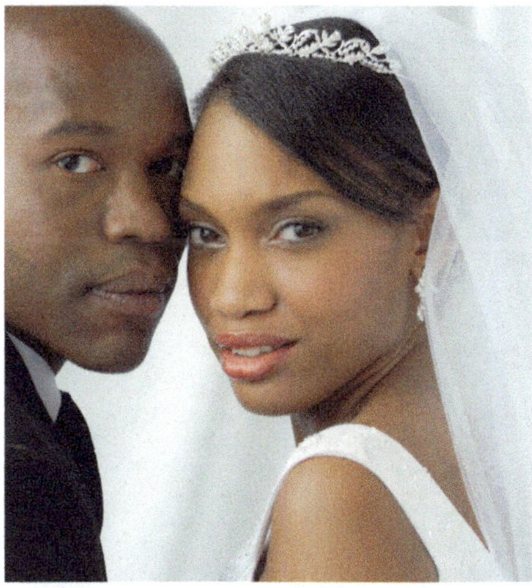

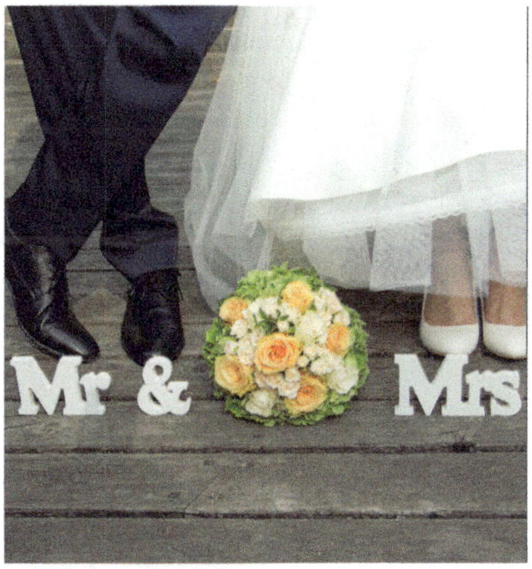
Mr & Mrs

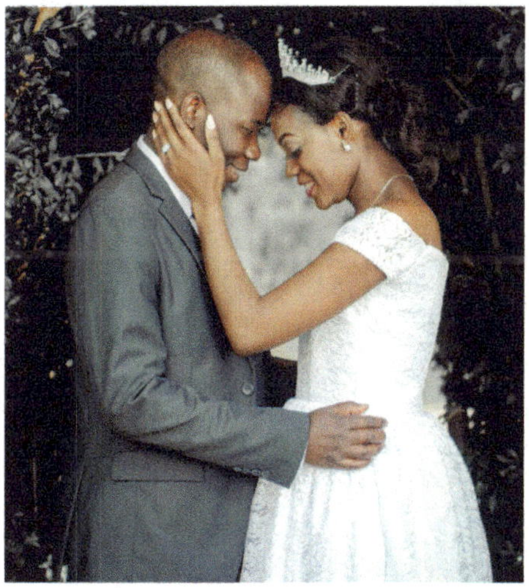

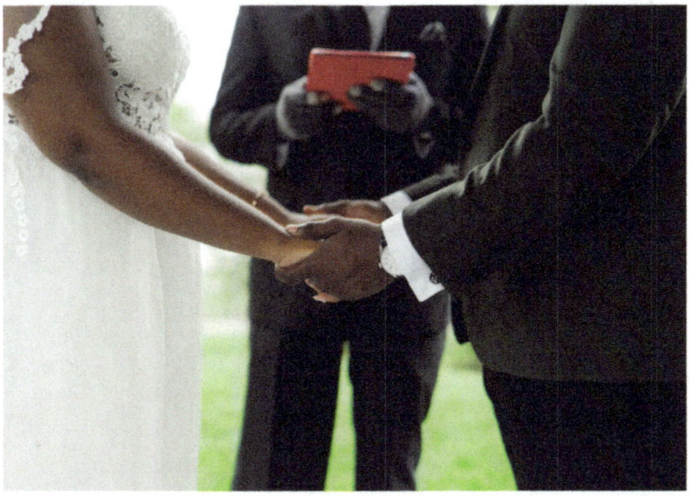

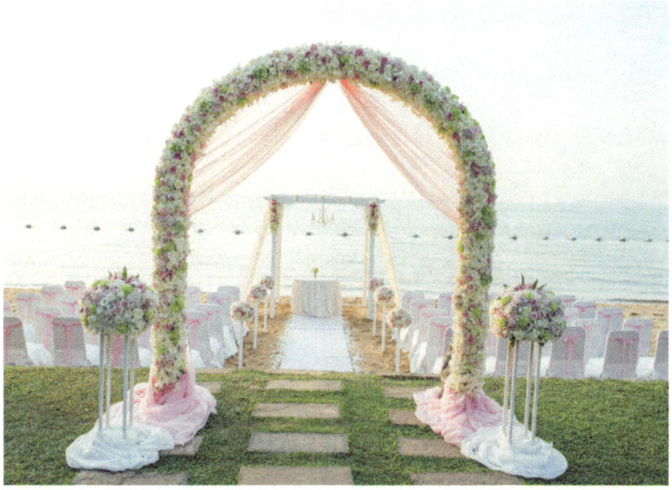

FRIENDS
never
FORGET
THE REAL FREINDS

TRUE
FRIENDS
ARE LIKE RARE GEMS,
PRECIOUS & HARD TO FIND.

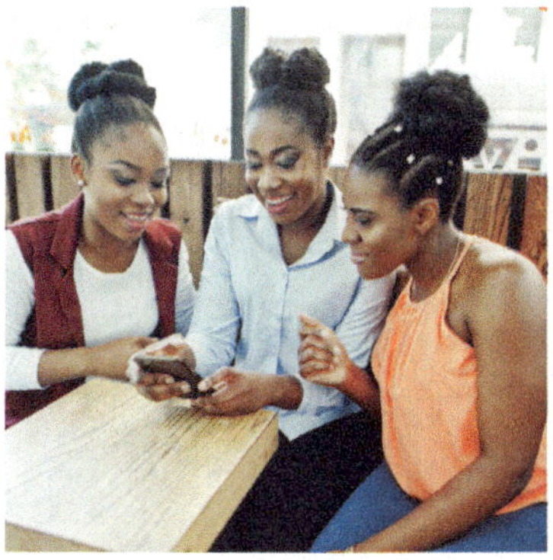
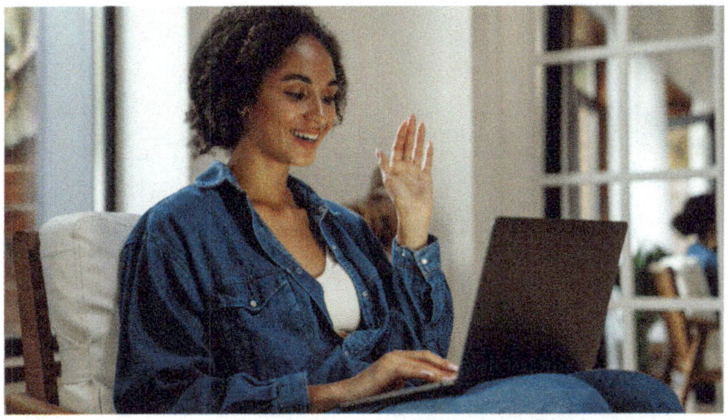
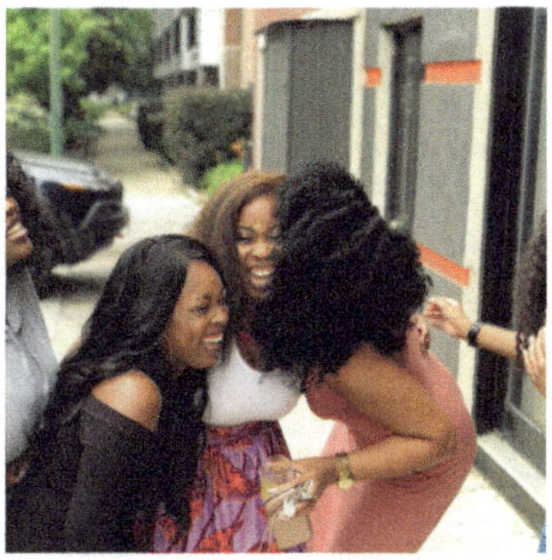
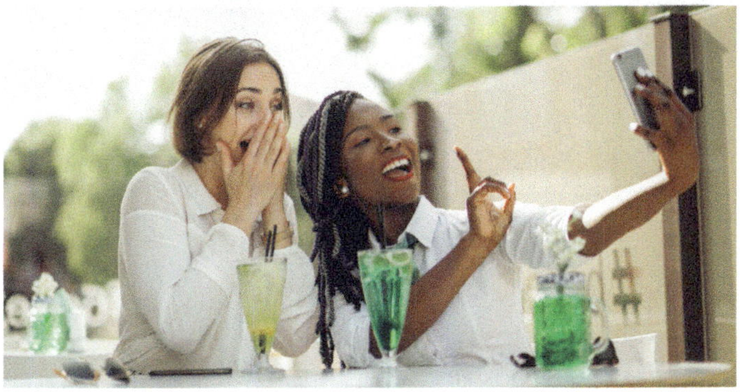
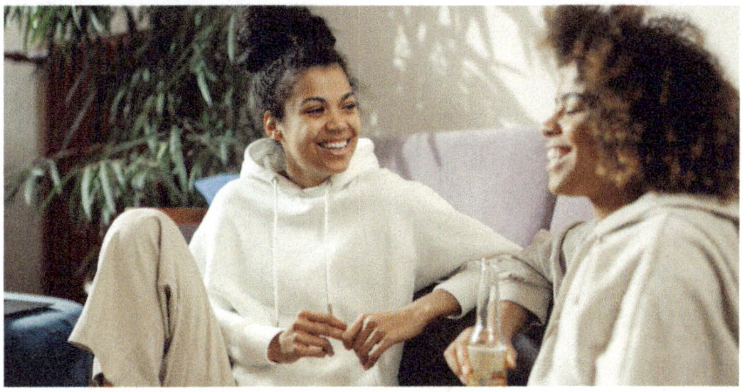
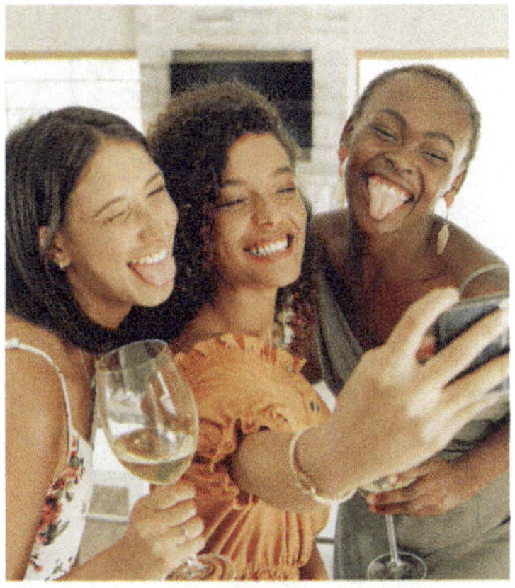
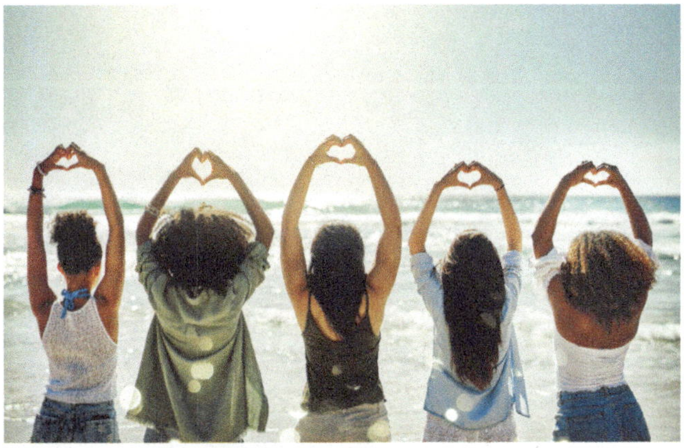
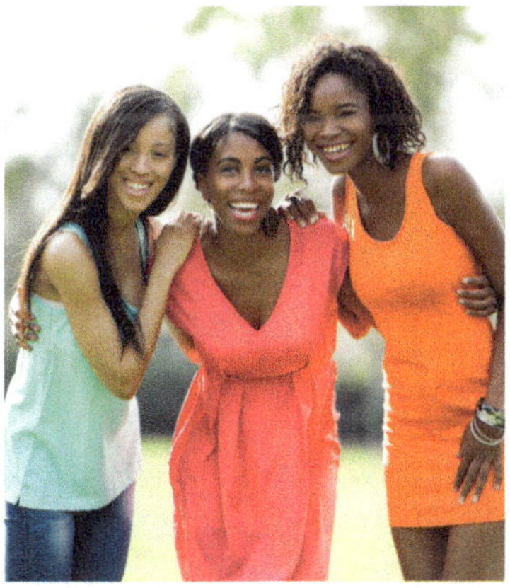
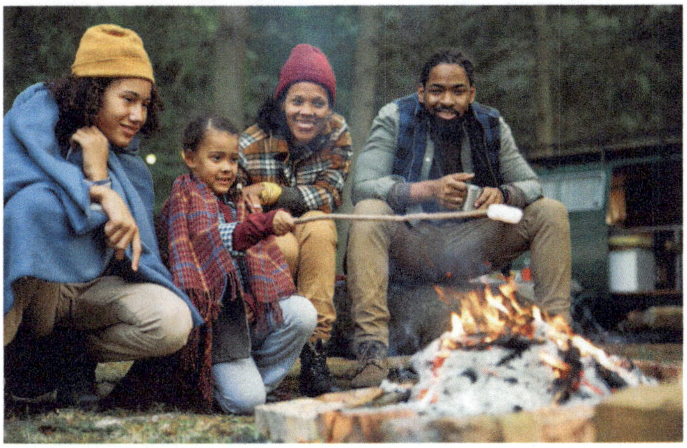
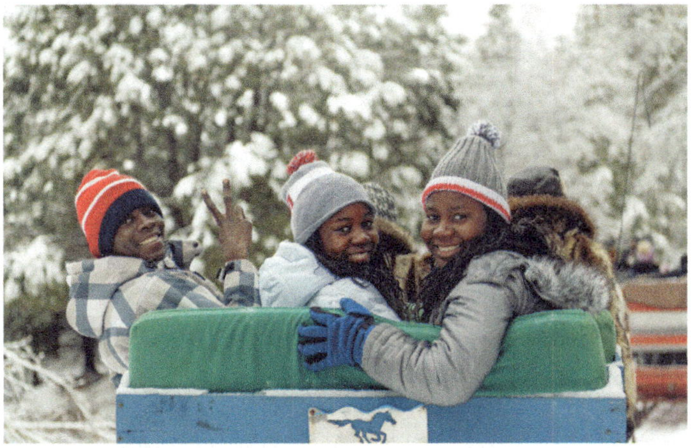

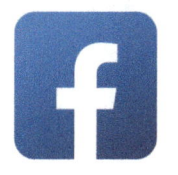

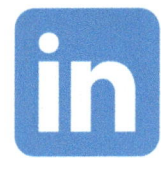

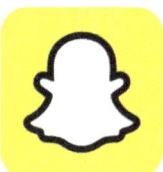

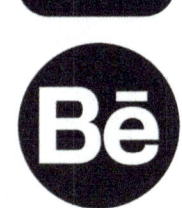

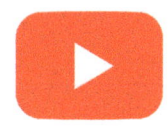

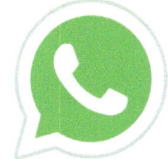

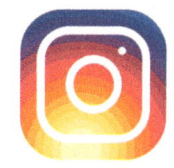

EVERY SPACE SHOULD **iNSPiRE** YOU TO LiVE YOUR BEST LiFE.

HODA

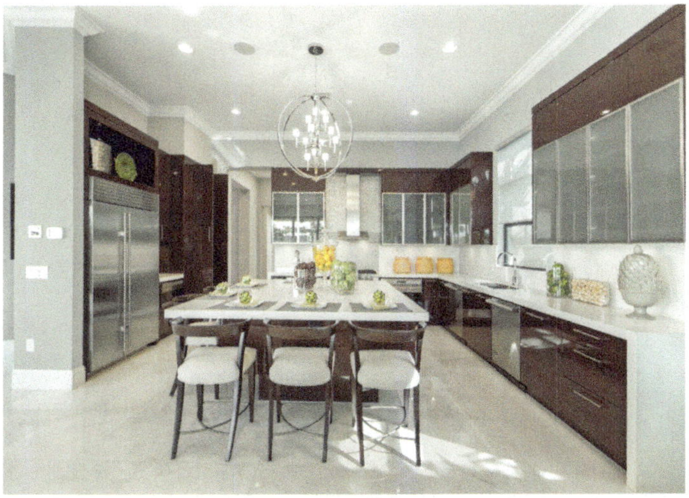
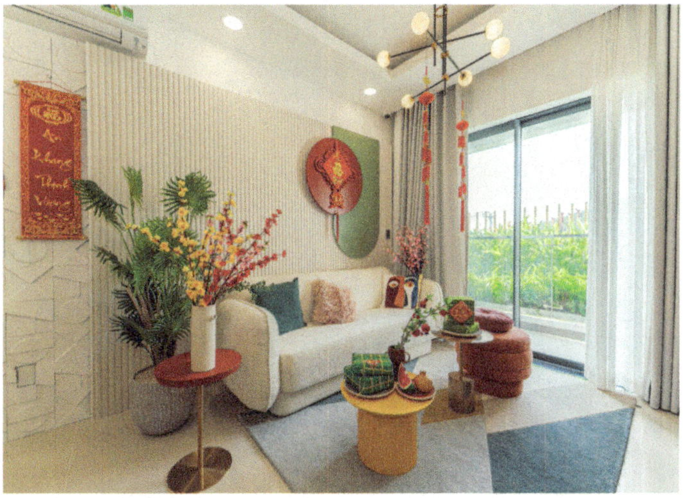
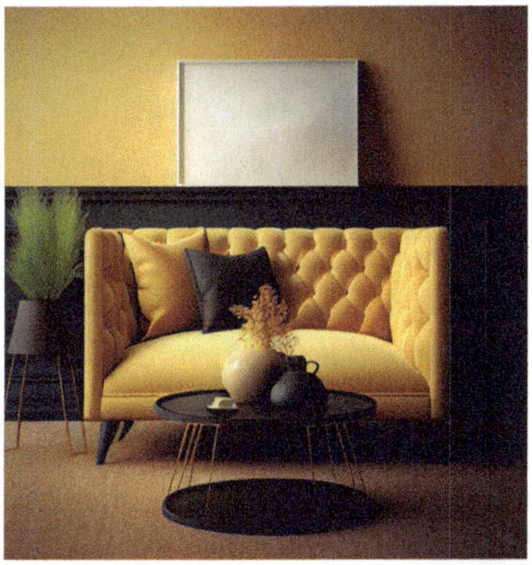
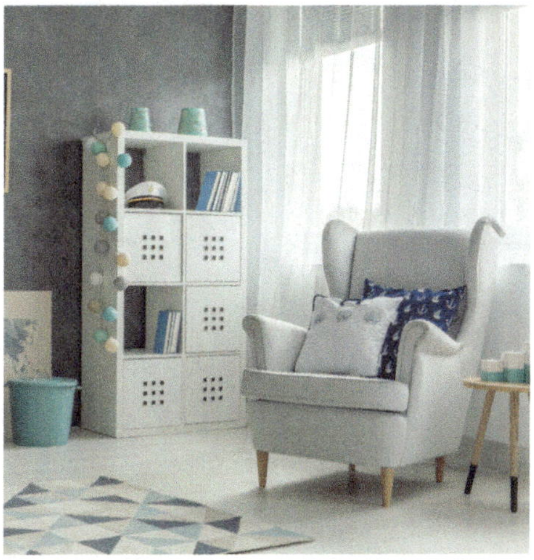
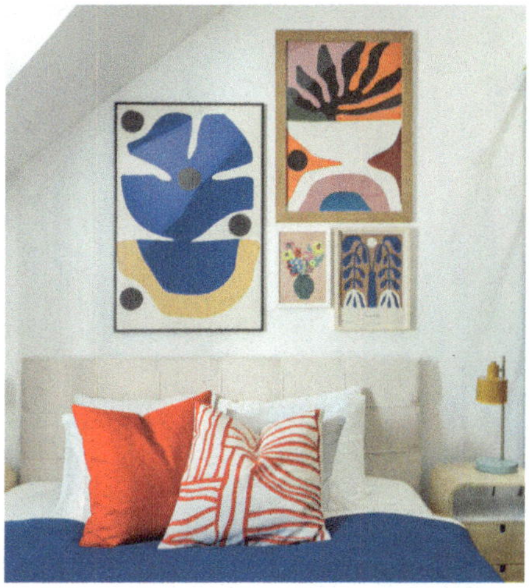
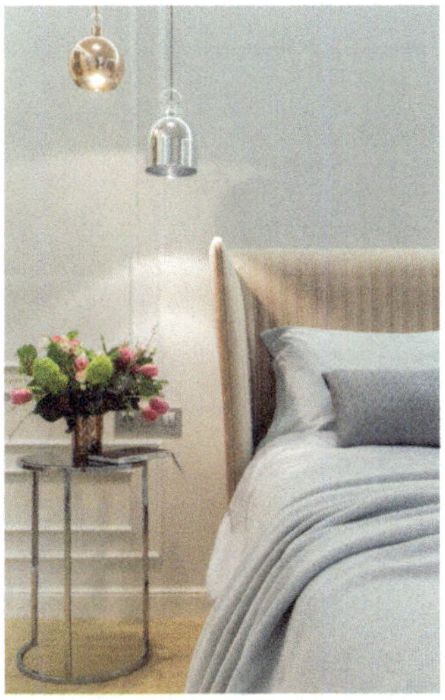
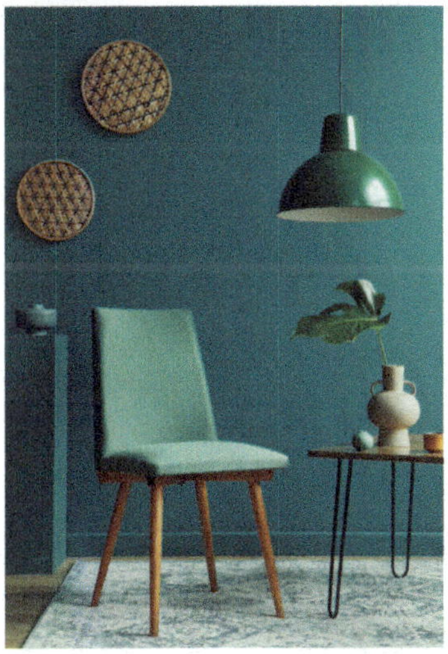
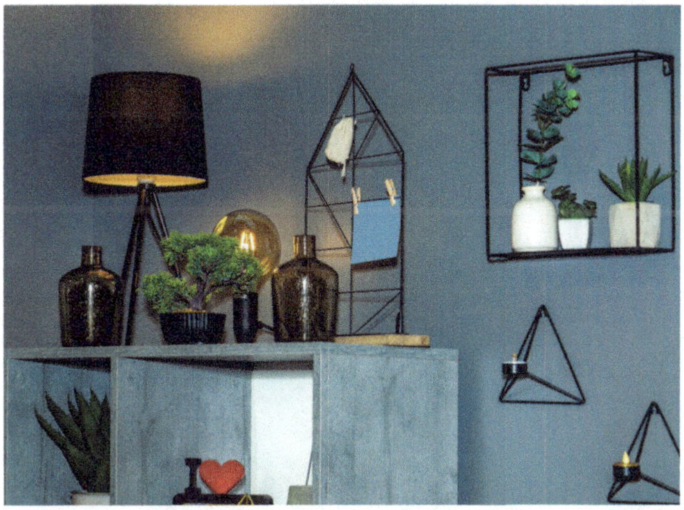
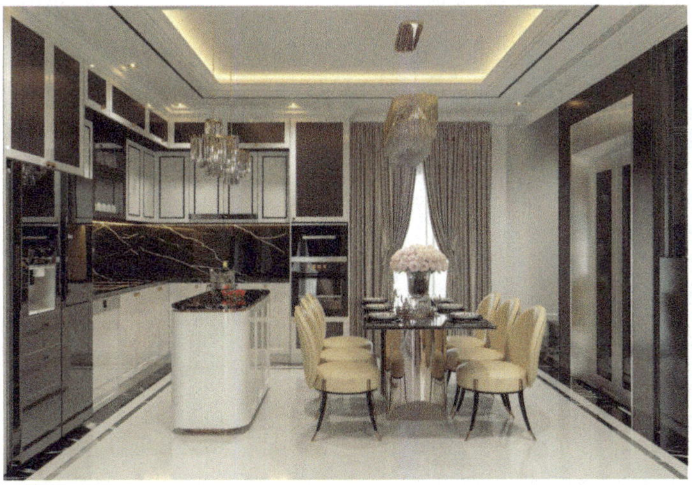
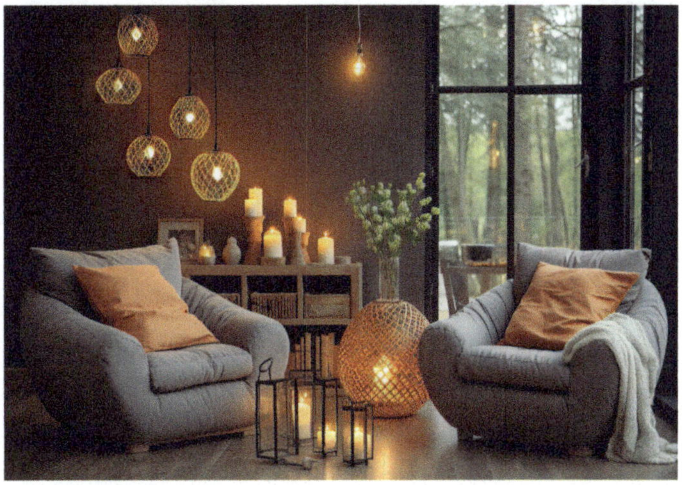

I AM

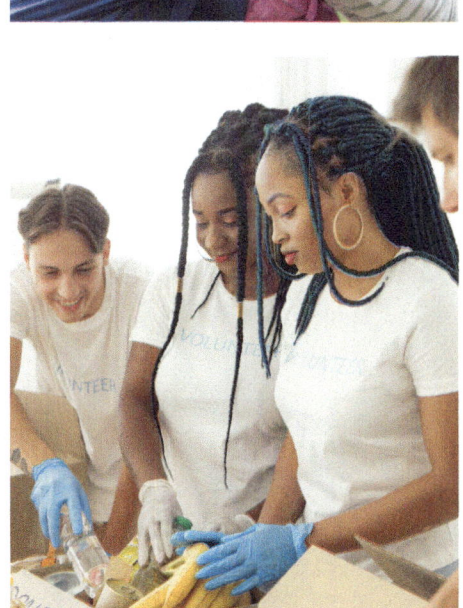

SURROUNDED BY A POWERFUL & SUPPORTIVE

COMMUNITY

WE DO NOT LIVE TO **WORK,** WE WORK TO **LIVE**

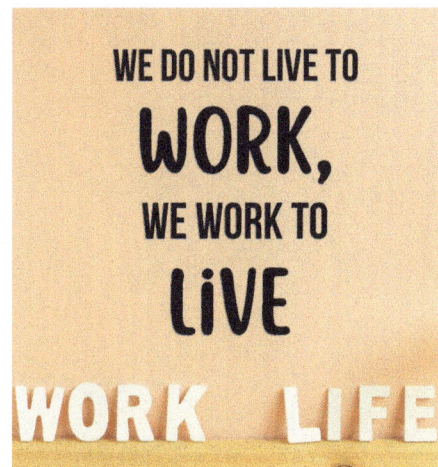

WORK LIFE

find harmony in your home, work and life

PEACEFUL PROGRESS

INNER GROWTH

HOBBIES

are great distractions from the worries and troubles that plague daily living.

BILL MALONE

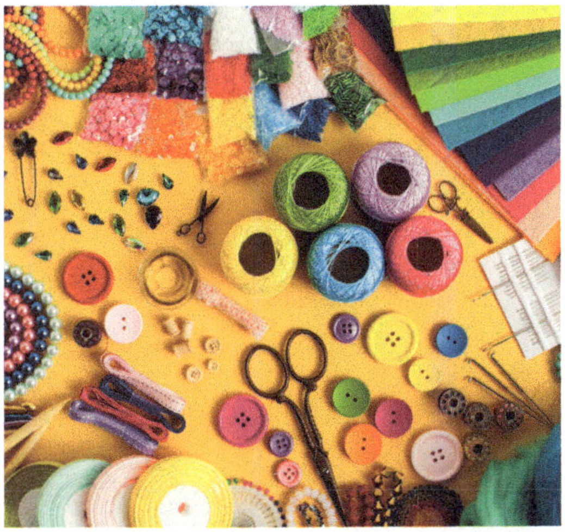
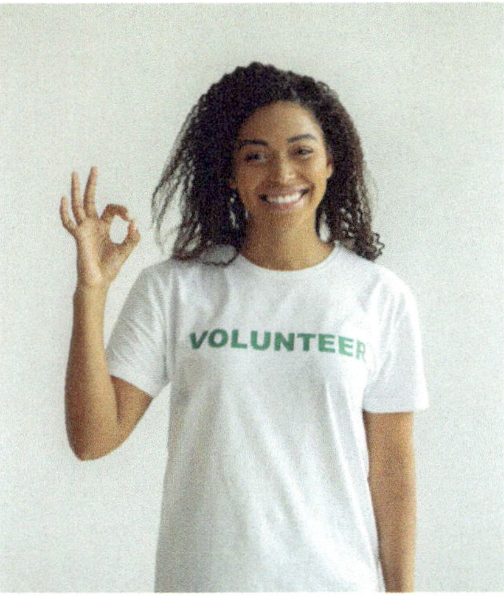
VOLUNTEER
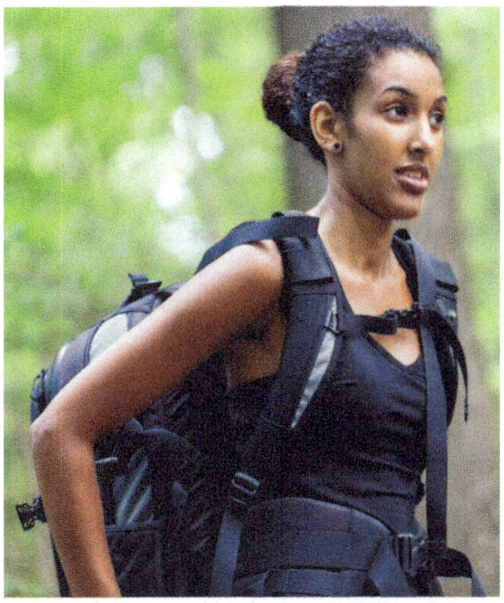
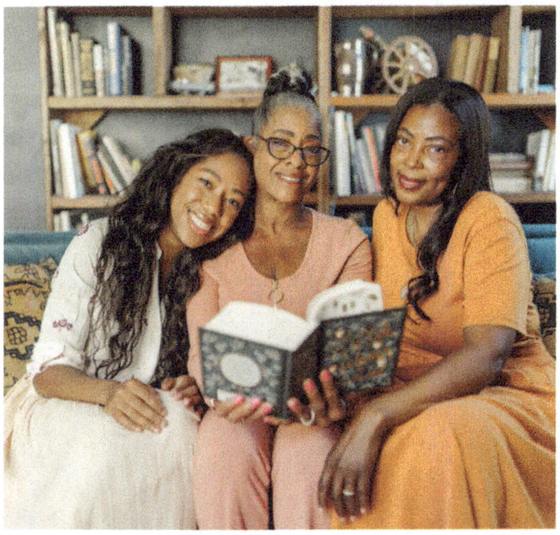
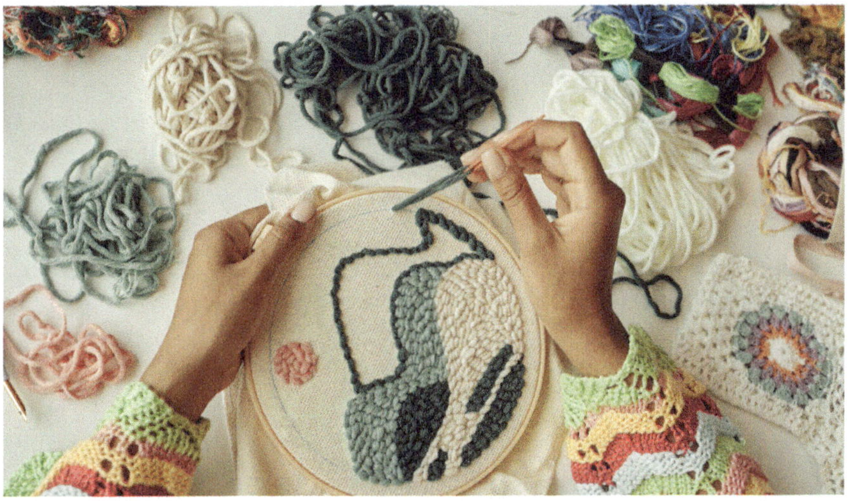
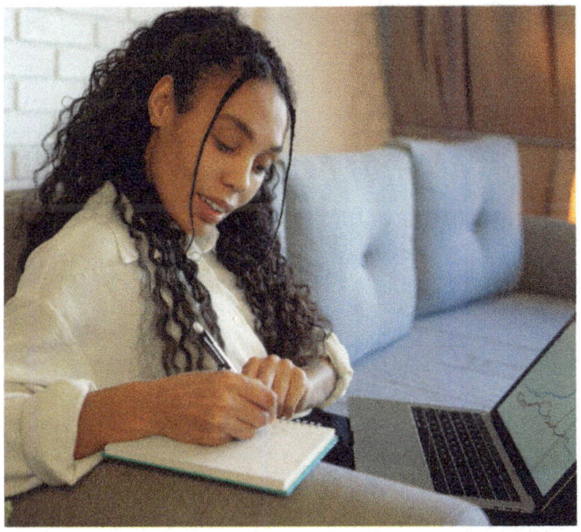
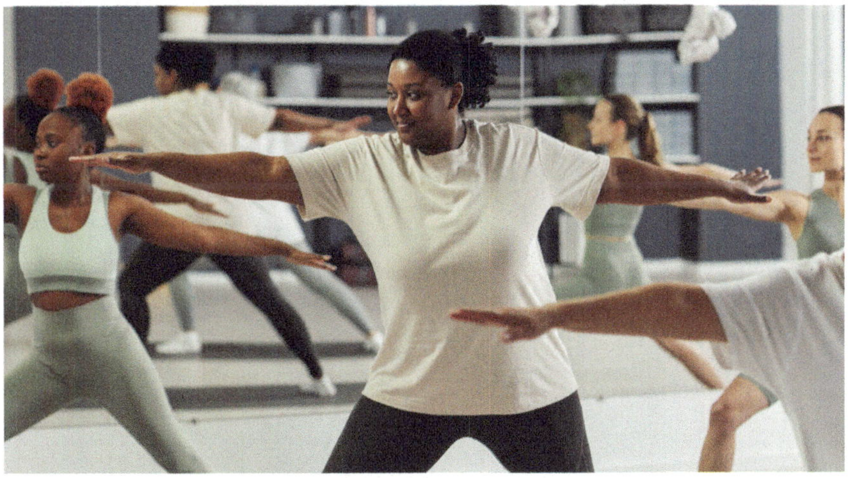
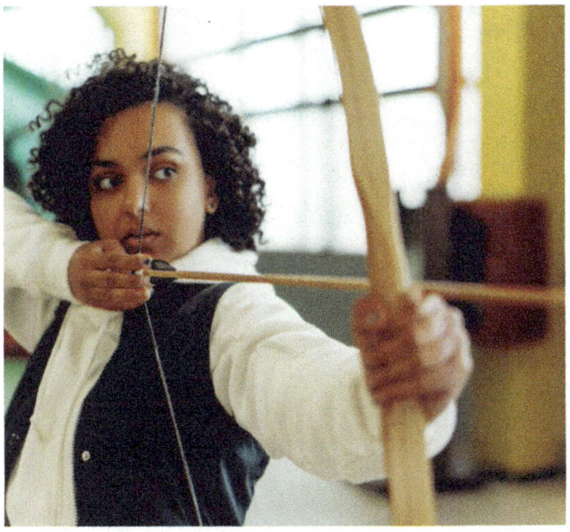
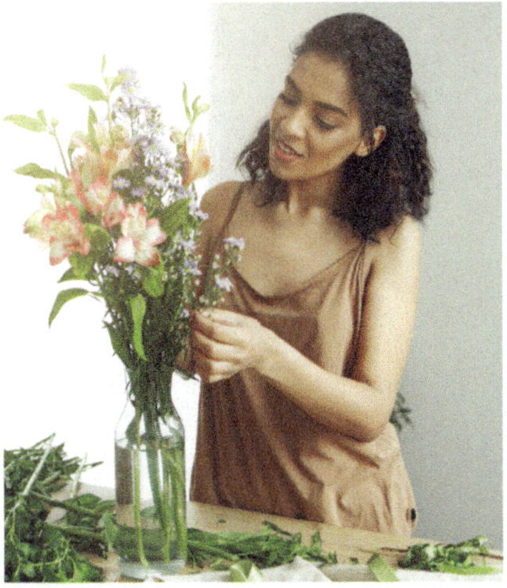
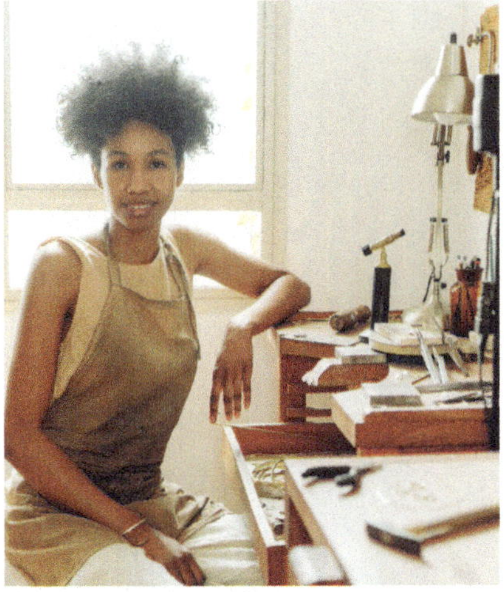

- I am UNIQUE
- I am MINDFUL
- I am LIMITLESS
- I am PROSPEROUS
- I am INSPIRED
- I am INFLUENTIAL
- I am BRILLIANT
- I am BLESSED
- I am VISIONARY
- I am BOLD
- I am ABUNDANT
- I am WORTHY

- Your mind is a weapon
- You're the greatest
- True love
- It's time to relax
- Love yourself more
- Behind every succesful woman is herself
- Create your own story
- Dream big never give up
- Happy Girls are the Prettiest
- Make yourself heard
- Smiles are always in fashion
- Selfcare is not selfish

- Be happy it drives people Crazy
- A reader lives a thousand lives
- Dream big and create your own story
- Selfie Queen
- GRL PWR
- Just believe in your dream
- The future is your motivation
- We wear crowns over here
- The present is your gift
- Happy girls are the prettiest
- Dream without fear and love without limits
- Happiness is not out there, it's in you

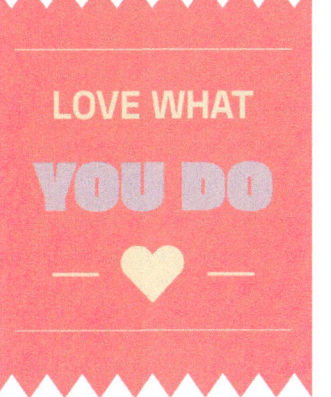

- Rest. Recover. Renew. Repeat.
- You Did It
- make it happen
- I am a queen
- Girl Power
- Love what you do
- You're Perfect
- be HAPPY
- keep your chin up
- Just find FREEDOM INSIDE YOUR MIND
- TAKE CARE OF YOURSELF
- TIME TO UPDATE!
- BELIEVE THEN BECOME
- it's A Beautiful day
- don't worry be happy
- Bloom with Grace
- You're Limited Edition
- Self love

- SUPER GREAT
- keep shining
- CREATIVITY TAKES COURAGE
- BE THE light
- GOOD work
- i honor my boundaries
- take time to rest your mind
- KEEP GROWING
- YOU ARE ENOUGH
- POSITIVITY is POWERFUL
- FAITH over FEAR
- NICE TRY!
- GOOD Vibes
- WHY AM I SO PERFECT?
- STRONGER TOGETHER
- UNBEETABLE!
- DON'T QUIT
- follow your dreams
- Loveliness inside
- IT'S okay TO cry
- You can do this
- be brave
- TROPICAL PARADISE
- Let's IMAGINE
- bad days don't stay bad forever
- make yourself a priority

Top Priorities

Financial Goals

Important Dates

Professional Goals

Savings Goals

Learning Goals

Things to Accomplish

Skills to Develop

Places for Travelling

Books for Reading

Habits to Develop

Things to Try

AAABBBCCCDDD
EEEFFFGGGHHH
IIIJJJKKKLLLMMM
NNNOOOPPPQQQ
RRRSSSTTTUUU
VVVWWWXXXYY
ZZZ111222333444
555666777888
999000@@@###***
!!!((()))<<<>>>
+++===???&&&
%%%$$${{}[[]

THANK YOU!

Thank you for bringing your aspirations to life with these inspiring visuals and your creative energy. We appreciate you embracing this empowering journey of visualizing your dreams through the pages of this book. May the focused intention you've poured into your vision boards continue to fuel your drive and propel you towards your goals.

If you're feeling motivated, scan the QR code to share how crafting these vision boards has expanded your perspective or ignited your passion. Your story about the transformative experience of visualizing your aspirations could inspire and encourage others embarking on their own journey of self-discovery and personal growth.

Made in the USA
Las Vegas, NV
24 February 2025